Fantastic FEATS AND FAILURES

by the Editors of *YES Mag*

Kids Can Press

To our Casey girl and to baby Remy, the new boy on the block — S.H. & D.G.

To my dad, who knows how to "build" a great story — J.I.

Acknowledgments

The authors would like to thank the following for reviewing portions of the text. Their assistance was much appreciated: Dr. Peter C. Birkemoe, Professor of Civil Engineering, University of Toronto; Dr. John B. Burland, Professor of Civil and Environmental Engineering, Imperial College London; Dr. Ron Graham, engineering consultant and instructor at the College of New Jersey; Simone Garneau, space consultant and co-founder of Futuraspace.

YES Mag is a bimonthly science magazine dedicated to introducing kids to science, technology and engineering in a fun and educational way. Visit us on the Web at www.yesmag.ca or send us mail at book@yesmag.ca.

The YES Mag team members who worked on this book are David Garrison, Shannon Hunt and Jude Isabella.

Photo Credits

Every reasonable effort has been made to trace ownership of and give accurate credit to copyrighted material. Information that would enable the publisher to correct any discrepancies in future editions would be appreciated.

Abbreviations

t = top; b = bottom; c = center; l = left; r = right

Cover photograph: Photos.com

p. 1: Manuscripts, Special Collections, University Archives, University of Washington Libraries, UW21422. PH Coll. 290.36; **p. 3:** (t, b) Photos.com, (c) Library of Congress; **p. 5:** (l) Photos.com, (r) Corbis/Magmaphoto.com; **p. 6:** (l) Photos.com, (r) Courtesy CN Tower — Canada's Wonder of the World; **p. 7:** (both) NASA; **p. 8:** (t) Kevin Fleming/Corbis/Magmaphoto.com, (b) Photos.com; **p. 10:** Hulton-Deutsch Collection/Corbis/Magmaphoto.com; **p. 11:** (all) Photos.com; **p. 12:** Photos.com; **p. 13:** Photos.com; **p. 14:** Courtesy Simpson Guppertz & Heger Inc.; **p. 15:** (both) Photos.com; **p. 16:** Photos.com; **p. 17:** (both) Photos.com; **p. 18:** (t) Bettmann/Corbis/Magmaphoto.com, (b) Photos.com; **p. 19:** Photos.com; **p. 20:** Courtesy Michele Sardy; **p. 22:** Courtesy HowardModels.com; **p. 23:** (t) Corbis/Magmaphoto.com, (c) Photos.com, (b) NOAA; **p. 24:** (t, c) Copyright Eurotunnel, (b) Photos.com; **p. 25:** (all) Copyright Eurotunnel; **p. 26:** Manuscripts, Special Collections, University Archives, University of Washington Libraries, UW20731. PH Coll. 290.39b; **p. 27:** Manuscripts, Special Collections, University Archives, University of Washington Libraries, UW21422. PH Coll. 290.36; **p. 28:** (t) Photos.com, (b) Library of Congress; **p. 29:** (l) Photos.com, (r) Library of Congress; **p. 30:** Photos.com; **p. 32:** Johnstown Museum; **p. 33:** Johnstown Museum; **p. 34:** Library of Congress; **p. 35:** Photos.com; **p. 36:** (t) Library of Congress, (b) Sergio Pitamitz/Corbis/Magmaphoto.com; **p. 37:** (t) Library of Congress, (b) Corbis/Magmaphoto.com; **p. 38:** Yann Arthus-Bertrand/ Corbis/Magmaphoto.com; **p. 39:** Baldev/Corbis Sygma/Magmaphoto.com; **p. 40:** (l, c) NASA, (r) Photos.com; **p. 41:** (both) NASA; **p. 42:** Canadian Space Agency; **p. 43:** (t) Canadian Space Agency, (b) NOAA; **p. 44:** NASA; **p. 45:** (t) NASA, (b) Photos.com; **p. 46:** Photos.com; **p. 47:** Photos.com; **p. 48:** Photos.com; **p. 49:** Photos.com; **p. 50:** Courtesy U.S. Air Force.

Kids Can Press acknowledges the financial support of the Government of Ontario, through the Ontario Media Development Corporation's Ontario Book Initiative; the Ontario Arts Council; the Canada Council for the Arts; and the Government of Canada, through the BPIDP, for our publishing activity.

Published in Canada by	Published in the U.S. by
Kids Can Press Ltd.	Kids Can Press Ltd.
29 Birch Avenue	2250 Military Road
Toronto, ON M4V 1E2	Tonawanda, NY 14150

www.kidscanpress.com

Edited by Val Wyatt
Designed by Julia Naimska
Illustrations by Jane Kurisu
Printed and bound in China by WKT Company Limited

The hardcover edition of this book is smyth sewn casebound. The paperback edition of this book is limp sewn with a drawn-on cover.

CM 04   0 9 8 7 6 5 4 3 2 1
CM PA 04   0 9 8 7 6 5 4 3 2 1

National Library of Canada Cataloguing in Publication Data

Fantastic feats and failures / by the editors of YES Mag ; illustrated by Jane Kurisu.

ISBN 1-55337-633-1 (bound).   ISBN 1-55337-634-X (pbk.)

1. Structural design — Juvenile literature. 2. Structural failures — Juvenile literature. 3. Structural analysis (Engineering) — Juvenile literature. I. Kurisu, Jane

TA149.F36 2004   j624.1'7   C2003-906974-5

Kids Can Press is a ꞁᴏʀᴜꜱ™ Entertainment company

CONTENTS

ENGINEERING

FEATS

FAILURES

To engineer is human! Engineering is the way we humans design and build everything from buildings and vehicles to bridges and towers. Sometimes we succeed — sometimes we fail.

Engineering feats can make the impossible possible. The Panama Canal, for example, lets ships travel "across land" from the Atlantic to the Pacific.

Everyone loves a feat, but it's the failures that grab the headlines. Lack of knowledge, poor design, bad safety practices, faulty materials and totally unexpected events can cause failures. Big or small, failures teach valuable lessons.

So, future engineers, grab your hard hats and steel-toed boots. And don't forget the blueprints. We're going up …

How did the Leaning Tower of Pisa get its lean? Turn to page 20.

CN Tower

It must be tempting, but so far no giant gorilla has climbed Toronto's CN Tower, the world's tallest building and Canada's wonder of the modern world.

What makes the 553.33 m (1815 ft., 5 in.) high tower an engineering feat are the three hollow "legs" that rise from its thick, Y-shaped base. To make the legs, engineers created a mold and attached it to the base. Cement was poured in and once it had hardened, hydraulic jacks lifted the mold higher, so that more concrete could be poured. Section by section, the tower rose.

Hydraulic jacks, forty-five of them, also lifted the Skypod (the donut at the top of the legs) into place. And because the tower was built as a communications hub, a 102 m (335 ft.) tall transmission mast was ferried to the top by helicopter.

Thanks to engineering ingenuity, the tower was completed in 1976 after forty months of hard work and $63 million. Today, the CN Tower is a world-renowned landmark that attracts two million visitors a year, has the world's highest restaurant, the longest metal staircase … well, you get the picture.

CHALLENGER

January 28, 1986, dawned clear and cold at Florida's Cape Canaveral. NASA's space shuttle *Challenger* was launching when tragedy struck. A mere 73 seconds into the flight, *Challenger* exploded, killing all seven astronauts aboard, including the first teacher in space, Christa McAuliffe.

What went wrong? Two Solid Rocket Boosters (SRBs) contain the fuel that lifts the shuttle into space. Each SRB has four sections. Two large rubber rings, called O-rings, close any gaps between the sections. Five seconds after lift-off, gray smoke puffed from an SRB joint. The O-ring was not sealing. Eventually a flame ignited *Challenger's* fuel supply, which exploded, ripping the spacecraft apart.

NASA engineers who worked on the shuttle knew the O-rings had been used over and over. They also knew that cold made the O-rings brittle. They had recommended postponing the flight. But managers had different priorities. They asked the engineers, "Are you certain that the O-rings will fail?" The answer was no. But the question should have been: "Can you be certain that the O-rings will not fail?"

After the tragedy, almost four hundred improvements were made to the shuttle program and for a while, all was well. But in 2003, tragedy struck again. The space shuttle *Columbia* broke apart on re-entry because of another engineering failure. Seven astronauts died, and NASA had to overhaul itself again.

A rubber O-ring like this one cracked and caused the Challenger *tragedy.*

GEORGIA DOME

There's No Place Like Dome

Domes have been used for hundreds of years, ever since some bright light figured that by repeating an arch, you got a large open space underneath.

The roof on Atlanta's Georgia Dome may be made of fabric, but it's so strong you could park a fully loaded pickup truck on it. (Not something we recommend.) Inside the Dome, 71 000 screaming fans can watch a football game with no columns to block the view. That's because the Georgia Dome, completed in 1992, is … well … a dome. And domes are engineering's elegant solution to the problem of putting a roof over a huge space without columns to hold it up.

The Georgia Dome's 114 fabric roof panels are stretched over a net of cables.

Early domes were made by filling in the triangular spaces between the arches with stone. But stone domes were heavy and there was a limit to their size. About three hundred years ago, builders switched to metal ribs, which were lighter than stone. The United States Capitol dome was built using cast iron ribs. But still, domes were heavy.

The United States Capitol dome is actually a dome within a dome. It's the outer dome that gives the building its impressive height.

Fifty years ago, American engineer-architect Buckminster Fuller came up with a dome that used interlocking triangles with a covering. Triangles are an engineering favorite because they are light — they're just three pieces with no center — yet stable shapes. When a heavy load is put on a triangle at one point, the sides transfer the load to the other points. A dome made of triangles is lightweight and strong.

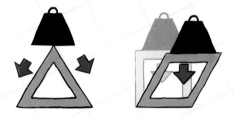

Set a heavy load on a triangle and it will not deform like a square will.

Dome, Sweet Dome

Like other domes, the Georgia Dome's roof is made of triangles. But these triangles are different — they're made from overlapping steel cables stretched tight.

Triangles plus tension is a great combo. The 35 000 m² (377 000 sq. ft.) fabric roof is draped over this net of cables and anchored at the edges. The result is a lightweight roof that covers a huge space and is, yes, strong enough to park a truck on.

- **Laid end to end, the supporting cables from the roof of the Georgia Dome would stretch 17.8 km (11.1 mi.).**
- **The thickest of the cables is only 10 cm (4 in.) in diameter.**
- **The Dome's center point is twenty-seven stories high.**

PROJECT: Goodie-Goodie Gumdrop Dome

Grab a box of toothpicks and thirty gumdrops and try making your own, low-tech dome.

1. Form a circular base by connecting five gumdrops with toothpicks as shown.

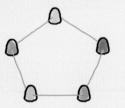

2. Make a triangle on one side of the base using two toothpicks joined at the top with a gumdrop.

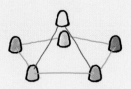

3. Repeat step 2 all the way around the base until you have five triangles.

4. Connect the gumdrops at the top of the triangles with toothpicks.

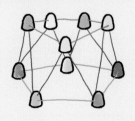

5. Insert toothpicks into each top gumdrop and angle them into the center. Use one gumdrop to connect them all.

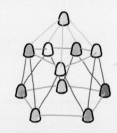

Congratulations — your dome is done. What would happen if you made a base of six gumdrops instead of five?

CRYSTAL PALACE

Imagine a curtain of glass hung from a steel frame. Big cities today are filled with buildings made of this curtain-wall construction — check out any skyscraper. But back in 1851, a big building made of glass was an oddity. The first large, glass structure was the Crystal Palace, built to house exhibitions for the first world's fair in London, England. And just about everything about the structure was new — or unique.

This photo, taken around 1854, shows the Crystal Palace after it was taken down and rebuilt.

A Smashing Success

More than two hundred designs for the fair's exhibit hall were rejected before landscape gardener and architect Joseph Paxton convinced officials to allow one more entry. While in a meeting, Paxton had hastily drawn a plan on blotting paper, using a giant water lily as inspiration.

It took only nine days to flesh out the plan. The public loved it, except one cantankerous government official who complained about the big elm trees about to go under the ax. So Paxton made room for the trees *inside* the Crystal Palace.

Then came the job of building the structure — all in less than six months. Enter the "assembly line." Parts for the palace were built elsewhere and shipped to the site in order of assembly — a new idea that saved time and money.

When the building's skeleton was complete, the glaziers (glass installers) began work. To make this part of the construction more efficient, Paxton designed a railcart big enough for four workers and a set of glass panes. The glaziers glided over these "rails," which were later recycled into gutters. Clever planning was evident everywhere. Even the construction site's wooden fences were reused, becoming floors and walls of the Crystal Palace.

Elm Trees and Sparrows

There was only one slight problem. Before the roof was finished, sparrows made the elm trees inside the building into comfy homes. Yikes! Bird droppings were everywhere. How to get rid of the sparrows? Guns? Bad idea. Poison? Didn't work. The solution came from the hero of the Battle of Waterloo, the Duke of Wellington. "Try sparrow hawks." It worked.

Gone But Not Forgotten

The Crystal Palace was never meant to be permanent, but its great success — more than 6 million visitors during the 141 days it was open — gave it a reprieve. It was dismantled and reassembled in another part of London. In 1936, it burned down.

Still, its legacy lives on. Tall buildings today are stiffened against the wind by attaching trusses and girders at the top and bottom of iron support columns, just like Paxton did. And the palace's walls — hung like curtains from the structural frame — foreshadowed the curtain walls of glass on today's skyscrapers.

- **The Crystal Palace had 293 655 glass panes. One worker installed 108 panes in just one day!**
- **4500 t (5000 tn.) of iron and 1700 m³ (60 000 cu. ft.) of glass were used to build the Crystal Palace.**
- **Dig through the topsoil in Hyde Park and you'll find the Crystal Palace's original footings.**

The Crystal Palace made glass and metal respectable as building materials. Today, we couldn't build skyscrapers without them.

SYDNEY OPERA HOUSE

The story behind the Sydney Opera House is so dramatic that someone wrote an opera about it, titled *The Eighth Wonder*. The building went $95 million over the (ridiculously low) original $7 million budget and took fifteen years to build. Moreover, the roof design was an engineering nightmare.

Architect Jørn Utzøn imagined the Sydney Opera House roof as a big ball divided like pieces of an orange.

On the Edge of the Possible

Architect Jørn Utzøn's simple, free-hand drawing was chosen out of 233 entries in an international competition. It featured amazing sail-like roofs at different angles. Australia wanted an icon, and Utzøn's vision was it.

Construction began in 1959, but soon hit a snag. A big snag.

No one knew how to build the opera house's revolutionary roof. Engineers spent about 350 000 hours (imagine one engineer working non-stop for forty years) on the unique technical problems posed by the roof design. For four years, they pushed computers to extremes trying to find a geometric solution to the roof. An acrylic and wood model was built and tested. But even it didn't answer the question: Will the foundation be strong enough to support such an elaborate and heavy roof?

Eureka

In a classic eureka moment, Utzøn found the answer. He told the engineers to imagine a big ball, divided like the pieces of an orange.

Instantly, the roof became a possibility, but could the foundation hold it up? Because construction had begun years before, the "guts" of the building were already in place, just waiting for the sail-like roof. But the roof's support columns would not support the redesigned roof's weight. So, every day when the construction crew left, a demolition team arrived to blow up a column. The next day, the crew began building another, stronger column in its place.

Delays and experiments cost money, and the costs were skyrocketing. Utzøn resigned in 1966, halfway through construction. He never saw his completed vision. In the end, however, Australia's goal was achieved — the Sydney Opera House, completed in 1973, is one of the most recognizable buildings in the world.

- More than 1 million white, ceramic tiles give the Sydney Opera House roof its gleaming finish.
- More than 350 km (220 mi.) of tensioned steel cable holds the roof sections together.

Situated on Bennelong Point in Sydney Harbour, the Sydney Opera House is now synonymous with Australia. But at the time, even its engineers thought it was impossible to build.

PROJECT: Reinforced Concrete

Under the trademark roof of the Sydney Opera House is a huge supporting structure made of reinforced concrete. This super-strong concrete is made by embedding steel rods into wet concrete. You may not have concrete at home, but you may be able to get some foam from a foam or craft store. To see how reinforcing adds strength, try this.

1. Cut a 5 x 5 x 50 cm (2 x 2 x 20 in.) piece of foam. This will be your concrete.

2. Hold the foam by one end. Does it bend under its own weight?

3. Put a piece of tape (the "steel rod") across the top and repeat step 2. Does the foam still bend?

The tape stops the foam from bending. The steel rod in reinforced concrete works in much the same way.

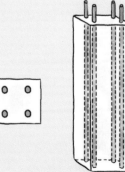

In reinforced concrete, the concrete resists "compression" while the steel rods resist "tension." For more about these forces, see page 15.

HYATT REGENCY HOTEL

Rod system attaches the third floor walkway to the ceiling.

Fourth floor walkway was here.

Second floor walkway was here.

Both walkways crashed to the floor.

More than 1500 people were in the lobby of the Hyatt Regency Hotel in Kansas City, Missouri, enjoying the weekly tea dance on the evening of July 17, 1981. While couples whirled around the dance floor, others socialized and watched. To get a better view, some spectators crowded onto the hanging walkways that overlooked the lobby at the second, third and fourth floors. Then out of the blue, there was "a big snap, like lightning in your backyard," as one witness described it.

In a matter of seconds, one of the worst structural failures in U.S. history had occurred. The fourth floor walkway suddenly collapsed onto the second floor walkway, sending both to the lobby floor. Concrete, metal, glass — and bodies — crashed down onto hundreds of people below. More than 200 people were injured and 114 died.

Causing a Catastrophe

Investigators easily spotted the problem. A metal rod that held the fourth floor walkway to the ceiling had failed. A freak accident? No. A simple, yet deadly, engineering error.

Engineering designs called for the second and fourth flour walkways to be attached to the ceiling by a row of long rods. Using these long rods was difficult, so the builder suggested a change: attach the fourth floor walkway to the ceiling by shorter hanging rods,

then use other rods to attach the second floor walkway to the fourth. It sounded like a small change, but it had big implications.

The change doubled the load of the fourth floor walkway. How? Suppose you and a friend both hung from a rope. That's how the original design was supposed to work. The rope supports you both. Now imagine holding onto the rope while your friend hangs onto your feet. Yikes — what a difference! The rope is supporting you, but you are supporting your friend. Eventually, you get tired and both come crashing down. That's basically what happened to the Hyatt's walkways. A project engineer approved the change by telephone — without a detailed check of the safety and load capacity of the redesign.

Ethics and Engineering

After the disaster, everyone pointed fingers at everyone else. After all, 120 engineers worked under the engineer of record (the supervisor) for the Hyatt Regency Hotel project. In the end, the engineer of record and the engineer who had approved the change by telephone lost their engineering licenses in the states of Missouri and Kansas.

The disaster also made the engineering profession change its procedures. The engineer of record is now totally responsible for the structural integrity of a project. He or she must give written approval for all contractor modifications.

INVISIBLE FORCES

Engineers pay close attention to two classes of force when designing anything — translational and rotational. These invisible forces stress materials and a structure must be designed with them in mind.

Translational forces move in a straight line. Tension, for example, is the pulling force. It stretches materials. The opposite of tension is compression, the pushing force. It squashes materials.

Rotational forces rotate. Torsion, for example, is a twisting force. It twists materials. Bending is the other rotational force.

Engineers must think about all the extreme forces and motions a structure must undergo. Wind, earthquakes and even gravity must be dealt with. They all cause structures to twist, bend, stretch and squash.

EIFFEL TOWER

When the German army rumbled into Paris in 1940, Adolph Hitler gazed up at the Eiffel Tower. He might have felt triumphant, but he'd have to walk up all 1710 steps to the top to rip down the French flag. For some "odd" reason the elevator had stopped working. France was occupied by the enemy — but not its heart, la tour Eiffel!

The Eiffel Tower was not always so loved. Artists and writers despised it, even calling it names — a tragic lamppost, a hollow candlestick, a dishonor to Paris!

A Lofty Idea with a Solid Base

Built in 1889 to commemorate the French Revolution's centennial and the Paris World's Fair, the Eiffel Tower was a disposable monument, meant to last a mere twenty years. But it turned out to be an enduring demonstration of engineering prowess.

Engineer Gustave Eiffel was well known for his bridge building. The tower, however, was something different. It would rise to untested heights — 300 m (1000 ft.) — making it the tallest structure in the world at the time.

Eiffel was most concerned with the effect of the wind at that height. Instead of a solid tower, he would use iron supports with enough open space between them to let most of the wind blow through. Eiffel calculated that even hurricane force winds wouldn't be able to topple his tower.

The metal girders weren't his only secret. He also designed a strong, four-legged base. Each leg would be 80 m (260 ft.) from the others and sit on a concrete foundation. But how to make a solid foundation on the waterlogged soil close to the Seine River?

To get around the problem, Eiffel used caissons — waterproof, iron-lined wooden boxes dug into the soil and filled with cement and rocks. When these foundations were in place, workers bolted the huge iron legs to them.

CAISSONS

Eiffel's caissons were enormous, iron-lined, wooden boxes with no bottom. Workers descended ladders into the caissons to shovel and pick out dirt and rocks, then the debris was scooped out and hauled up to the surface. As workers dug, the caissons sunk lower. When the caissons hit bedrock, fast-setting concrete was poured in. Limestone blocks were dumped in next, then more hard stone. The sixteen caissons became the tower's sturdy foundation.

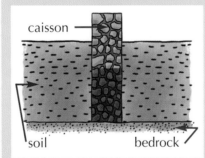

caisson

soil   bedrock

• The tower is protected from oxidation (rusting) by several layers of paint. It's been painted seventeen times, about once every seven years. It takes twenty-five painters a year to finish the job.

A Leg Up

Each leg was made up of four iron columns. The legs were on an angle and met at 55 m (180 ft.). This was where the first platform was to be built. But how to make the platform level? If even one leg was in the wrong position, the platform would be on a tilt, like a table with a wonkey leg. Eiffel used hydraulic jacks and pistons to raise or lower the legs — think of how a car is raised and lowered to change a tire. In this way, he could move the legs into just the right position. Then girders were bolted into place, joining the columns like a belt.

Tower Power

Eiffel had a blueprint for every metal piece used — 5329 mechanical drawings for 18 038 separate pieces. Every hole for the 2.5 million rivets was drawn in — vital, because only a third of the

These time-lapse photos show the Eiffel Tower going up.

rivets were made on site. The others were riveted at the factory.

Finished iron pieces arrived regularly by horse-drawn carts from Eiffel's shops 5 km (3 mi.) away. Pieces were lifted into position by tall, steam-powered cranes. Each girder weighed no more than 3 t ($3\frac{1}{3}$ tn.) — these "small" components made building faster and safer, even if it

meant more riveting. As the tower grew, the cranes were mounted on inclined tracks. The tracks would later be used for the elevators.

A twenty-one cannon salute marked the opening of the Eiffel Tower on March 31, 1889. It was ahead of schedule (built in just 21 months) and under budget, at 7.8 million francs. During the year of the fair, the tower had more than 1.9 million visitors.

Although the Eiffel Tower was meant to be torn down in 1909, the science, art and technology that went into it won peoples' hearts, and it was preserved. Today it is Paris's most famous landmark and a major communications hub. Not to mention a huge tourist attraction.

When you see the Eiffel Tower, you know you are in Paris.

Gustave Eiffel designed the Statue of Liberty's steel and iron skeleton.

GUSTAVE'S LASTING GLORY

Long before Gustave Eiffel built his tower, he had a solid reputation as an engineer of metal structures. He designed bridges and the Statue of Liberty's steel and iron skeleton.

He also had a lot of respect from the workers. He once dove into the Garonne River to save a worker who had fallen from a bridge. The tower was his last great success. He next signed a contract to build locks for the Panama Canal, but the French bid to build the canal failed, and Eiffel never got a chance to build his locks. (For more about the Panama Canal, see page 34.)

The last twenty years of his life were dedicated to scientific research, specifically aerodynamics. A wind tunnel he designed and built at the foot of the Eiffel Tower is still in use today. He died in 1923 while the Eiffel Tower was still the tallest human-made structure in the world.

LEANING TOWER OF PISA

What would Italy's Leaning Tower of Pisa be without the lean? Just like every other medieval tower in Europe!

Let's face it — medieval builders constructed a failure. Sure it's cool to look at, but towers aren't meant to lean. By 1990, the tower leaned so far that it seemed to defy gravity.

Tilt!

The tower was designed as a bell tower to complement Pisa's cathedral. Construction began in 1173 and ended five years later with only three stories built. The tilt to the south was noticeable even then.

The tower leans because it rests on the clay, fine sand and shells of an old riverbed. The tilt to the south happened because the sediments on that side compressed. But it wasn't the leaning that halted the project. Wars and lack of money kept stopping construction. That turned out to be a good thing because the long breaks allowed the sediments under the tower to settle and get stronger.

The Leaning Tower of Pisa leans 4 m (13 ft.) off center.

Work began again in 1272. To compensate for the lean, workers added heavier material to the tower's north side. Work stopped in 1278. The tower leaned even more — almost a meter (three feet)! Once again, the tower had time to settle.

In 1360, construction began on the tower's top section. Ten years later, the tower reached its final height of 60 m (200 ft.) — with an even bigger lean. Over the years, the tower's south side continued to sink and attempts to fix it just made the lean worse.

The Big Fix

In 1990, engineers were called in to perform an engineering feat to save the tower — and the lean. They got to work, but it was no easy task. In fact, the tower almost collapsed in 1995. Then the engineers convinced officials that an earlier idea could be made to work — soil extraction.

They drilled a total of forty-one holes under the tower's foundation on the north side. Only six holes were drilled at a time, however. Overnight, the tower settled and sealed the holes. The engineers decided which holes to extract soil from on a daily basis. They were literally "steering" the tower.

Lovin' the Lean

On December 15, 2001, the Leaning Tower was officially re-opened. The lean was reduced by only ten percent — unnoticeable to the human eye. But engineers expect this small adjustment to keep the tower safe, stable — and leaning — for another three hundred years.

- Engineer John Burland worked, on average, two days a week for eleven years to save the Leaning Tower of Pisa. He was the guy "steering" the tower.
- The Leaning Tower of Pisa weighs about 14 500 t (16 000 tn.). That's a lot of weight to steer.

PROJECT: Towering Edible Edifice

How sky-high can you build a tower of uncooked spaghetti and marshmallows?

Do whatever you want with the materials. Build your tower as high and as strong as you can. How much weight will your tower support? Will it hold a ping-pong ball? A golf ball? A tennis ball? A basketball? Try using a fan or a hairdryer to see how wind affects your structure.

CITICORP BUILDING

Engineer William LeMessurier faced a big challenge in designing the Citicorp Building in New York City — he had to build a skyscraper *in the air*. The land Citicorp wanted to build on was owned by St. Peter's Church. The church made a deal with Citicorp — St. Peter's would give Citicorp "air space" above the church, if Citicorp built a new church to replace the old one. In effect, the Citicorp building would have to be on ten-story "stilts" above the street. The church, however, was at the corner of the lot. That meant the support columns for the skyscraper had to be located in the middle of the building, rather than at the corners.

LeMessurier's design featured four massive columns. The structure would be stable, except for the swaying that all tall structures experience in high winds. A 400 t (440 tn.) concrete slab would be set on top of the building. It would be connected by a shock absorber to the building to counteract the swaying. A system of 48 arrow-shaped wind braces would be installed in the outside walls to resist the force of the wind.

The design was successfully tested in a wind tunnel. The bulldozers and cranes moved in. A dilapidated old church vanished, and in its place emerged a church with a soaring, 59 story high skyscraper perched above it. All was well. Until …

Uh-oh!

A year after construction was completed in 1977, an engineering student phoned to ask LeMessurier some questions about the design. After confidently explaining why it worked, LeMessurier decided to review his original plans. That was when he noticed something.

When the skyscraper was built, a design change had been made — the special wind braces were bolted together, not welded. As LeMessurier recalculated wind factors, he realized that the bolted joints were too weak to withstand high winds. A violent storm sweeping in from a certain direction could topple the Citicorp Building, and hurricane season was on its way.

914' Tall

The Stubbins Assoc

Saving the Skyscraper

Something had to be done and fast. LeMessurier ordered 5 cm (2 in.) thick plates welded over the bolted joints to strengthen them.

Work began immediately. Welders fixed the joints from inside after ripping away the surrounding flooring and walls. The work went on at night so it wouldn't bother the tenants.

Still, weather reports of hurricanes battering the Caribbean were an ominous sign. Citicorp owners wanted the repair work to go on twenty-four hours a day. But smoke from the welding would set off the building's smoke detectors, so work continued only at night.

Then came Hurricane Ella, headed right for New York City. On the morning of September 1, meteorologists reported that Ella would probably arrive later that day. Would Citicorp survive Ella?

We'll never know. Hurricane Ella changed course, blowing away from Manhattan. And a couple of weeks later, the Citicorp repairs were done. The building, with its trademark slanted roof and "stilts," still stands proudly, now a familiar part of the Manhattan skyline.

Hurricane Ella

EUROTUNNEL

The Eurotunnel is actually three tunnels — two for trains and one for service vehicles.

Breakthrough! French and English workers exchanged flags when their tunnels met for the first time.

Nicknamed the Chunnel (short for Channel Tunnel), the Eurotunnel is the longest underwater tunnel in the world. It links England and France 45 m (147 ft.) below the surface of the English Channel.

Building the Chunnel was a massive undertaking.

It took 13 000 engineers, technicians and workers six years and about $21 billion to do it. And it took some really big machines — the eleven specially designed Tunnel Boring Machines,

or TBMs, were each as long as two football fields end to end.

The TBMs began to chew through the chalky earth below the English Channel in 1988. At a rate of 75 m (250 ft.) a day, they weren't setting any speed records. To make things more exciting, the British and French tunnelers had a race to see who could get to the halfway point first. The British won, but, to be fair, the French faced tougher conditions.

Engineers, however, were the big winners. If the tunnelers had been more than 2.5 m (8 ft.) out of line, the two sides would have just tunneled past each other.

A Record Breaker

The Chunnel is actually three concrete-lined parallel tunnels that run for 38 km (24 mi.) under the English Channel. There's another 12 km (7.5 mi.) at either end, for a total of 50 km (31.5 mi.).

Trains carrying passengers and vehicles zoom through the two outside tunnels, which are both 7.6 m (25 ft.) in diameter. The tunnels are one way, so there's no risk of collisions. Worries about fire and other catastrophes led engineers to design a middle tunnel, called the service tunnel. It's narrower and connected every 375 m (1230 ft.) to the rail tunnels with crossover passages. Two huge crossover "caverns" allow trains to switch tracks if needed.

The tunnels are amazing, but only a part of the package.

A cooling system — chilled water pumped through pipes — keeps tunnel temperatures down. Five pumping stations keep the tunnel puddle-free. And an electrical system keeps things moving.

In 1994, the first trains whisked through the tunnels at 160 km/h (100 m.p.h.). The trip across the English Channel was reduced from a ninety-minute ferry ride to an easy twenty-minute trip.

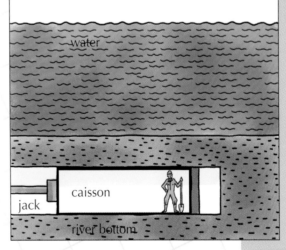

To build the Thames Tunnel, workers dug out a space behind the removable end wall (in red). The jack pushed the caisson ahead, into the empty space. Then the process was repeated.

A Shipworm, a Tunnel, an Idea

Marc Isambard Brunel began to build the world's first underwater tunnel, under the Thames River, in 1825. Brunel invented a tunnel shield, inspired by the "shields" shipworms use. (Shipworms are worms that burrow into wood on ships.) The invention was like a backless iron box with removable wooden planks in the front. Diggers inside removed a plank and dug out as much as possible then replaced the plank. Hydraulic jacks then pushed the iron box forward, and the process was repeated. The muddy walls were lined with bricks.

Five times the planks failed and the tunnel flooded. Methane in the soil caused explosions. No wonder the tunnel took eighteen years to complete! But the Thames Tunnel remains — it's part of London's subway system.

TACOMA NARROWS BRIDGE

The Tacoma Narrows Bridge connecting Washington State's Olympic Peninsula to the mainland across Puget Sound was a worry from the start. It swayed and rolled so much when it opened on July 4, 1940, that drivers would lose sight of cars ahead of them on the bridge. No wonder it was nicknamed Galloping Gertie.

Snap and Sway

The bridge's engineer Leon Moisseiff was well respected. He had been a consulting engineer for the famous Golden Gate Bridge and other suspension bridges. But in this bridge design, he neglected an important factor — aerodynamics, or how wind flows around an object.

A man runs to safety moments before the bridge collapses.

Four months after the Tacoma Narrows Bridge opened, on November 7, a 67 km/h (42 m.p.h.) wind sent the bridge into a heavy sway. Suddenly, the cables on the west side snapped. Officials closed the bridge, which was now dancing out of control.

• **In 1940, Galloping Gertie was the third longest suspension bridge in the U.S., with a main span of 853 m (2800 ft.) Today the world record is Japan's Akashi Kaikyo Bridge, with a main span of 1991 m (6532 ft.).**

Pushing Bridge Boundaries

Suspension bridges have two main components, cables and towers. The cables are draped over the towers and anchored to huge concrete blocks on the shore. The roadway and cars pull down on the cables, which transfer this load to the towers and concrete blocks. The cables also help to stabilize the roadway, but suspension bridges can still sway in the wind and wobble with the movement of cars. So extra trusses (reinforcing braces) are needed.

Moisseiff pushed engineering design boundaries because he used a solid steel girder for strength instead of the stiffening trusses. The result was a slender, but flexible bridge — that rolled and twisted. A lot.

Right after it opened, University of Washington engineers began studying the bridge and attempts were made to fix it. Meanwhile, news of the roller-coaster bridge spread, and motorists cruised over Galloping Gertie for a thrill. The engineers kept trying to stop the motion. Cables and plate girders were connected to 50 t (55 tn.) concrete blocks for more stability. But nothing worked. The cables broke on November 7 and the bridge tumbled into the water below. Legend has it that the only casualty was Tubby, a dog left in a car while the owner crawled to safety.

Why Gertie Fell

Investigations revealed a number of things. The design and workmanship were fine. However, Moisseiff's innovative design lacked the stiffness required to resist the winds. Today, engineers use wind tunnels to test bridge designs before construction starts. They want their bridges to be stable, not "galloping."

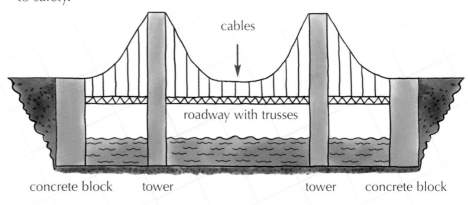

A typical suspension bridge with reinforced trusses.

BROOKLYN BRIDGE

It was winter 1852. Engineer John Roebling was crossing the East River between Brooklyn and Manhattan on a ferry — it was the only way to make the trip. He was with his son, Washington, and he was impatient because the ferry was stuck in ice. What if a bridge could be built in this very place? His dream for a bridge was born.

THE GREAT EAST RIVER SUSPENSION BRIDGE

Suspending Belief

The idea for a bridge wasn't new, but the distance across the river — about half a kilometer (a third of a mile) — seemed too great to span. If it could be built, the bridge would be the longest in the world. And the river was a busy shipping channel, so a bridge would have to be high enough to let even the tallest ships pass under it.

By 1869, John Roebling, who had already designed three suspension bridges, came up with a daring plan. He would use four thick, steel cables — rather than the iron cables used at the time — draped over massive towers to create the bridge.

Unfortunately John didn't live to see the start of construction. A ferry slammed into a pier while he was surveying the river and crushed his foot. Infection set in and he died less than a month later. The chief engineer's job fell to his son Washington.

- Each of the four main cables contained 5600 km (3500 mi.) of steel wire. The wires in one cable, if laid end to end, would stretch from Brooklyn to Los Angeles.
- On opening day, pedestrians paid a penny each to cross the bridge. Vehicles were charged five cents.
- In 1884, P.T. Barnum led a herd of twenty-one elephants across the Brooklyn Bridge.

The Foundation and the Towers

Building the towers from which the cables could be hung was Washington Roebling's first job. As with the Eiffel Tower, the builders needed to deal with a soggy river bottom. Once again, they used caissons (see page 17). When the caissons hit bedrock, they would be filled with concrete and rock.

The bridge's two towers, made of granite, were set on top of the caissons to help drive the caissons downward. The towers soar 84 m (276 ft.) above the water, taller than any Manhattan building at the time. Their main job is to hold up the steel cables, all 12 000 t (13 225 tn.) of them, and to hold the roadway high enough for ships to pass under.

The Cables

Washington Roebling knew steel was stronger than iron and certainly stronger than rope. But the steel cables for the Brooklyn Bridge would have to be super strong. They would have to hold up four lanes of traffic, plus a

Today, about 144 000 vehicles cross the Brooklyn Bridge daily.

railway line. Steel cables had never ever been tried on bridges. Would they work?

To make each of the four main cables, 278 steel wires were tied together in a bundle called a strand, and then nineteen of these strands were wrapped together. When finished, the cables measured 40 cm ($15\frac{3}{4}$ in.) in diameter.

The cables were anchored to land on both shores, then draped over the towers. Smaller, vertical cables hung down from the main cables. It was to these vertical cables that the roadway was attached. Still more cables reinforced the bridge, adding extra strength.

Attaching the cables was a dangerous job. Occasionally a strand broke loose — once decapitating a worker. During the fourteen years of construction,

more than twenty men died working on the Brooklyn Bridge.

When completed, the Brooklyn Bridge soared across the East River. The bridge would prove to be an amazing feat — and an enduring landmark — but it got off to a rocky start. A week after its official opening in May 1883, 20 000 people surged across the bridge during Memorial Day festivities. Someone screamed and panicked the crowd. Twelve people were trampled to death.

CAISSON DISEASE

Compressed air pumped into a caisson made the air unbearably hot and humid. And the farther down the caisson went, the more the increased pressure made it difficult to breathe. Aside from discomfort, the work could be fatal. Men actually died of "caisson disease."

Caisson disease is what we now call "the bends," something scuba divers are susceptible to. Every day caisson workers climbed from the pressurized air in the caisson to the normal air pressure outside. Their bodies needed time to adjust. If they came to the surface too quickly, nitrogen, which is normally expelled by the body, built up in their bloodstream and made them sick. Nitrogen bubbles in the bloodstream can also lodge in the brain, lungs or spinal cord. During construction, Washington Roebling himself suffered from caisson disease and was left paralyzed. His wife, Emily, became his eyes, ears and voice in the Brooklyn Bridge project.

PROJECT: Build a Bridge

Drive from one end of a country to another and you'll see all kinds of bridges. Whether a beam, arch, truss, cantilever or suspension bridge, all bridges have three things in common: a deck, supports and foundations. Make a simple bridge yourself.

You'll need:

- 5 sheets of newspaper
- 25 paper clips
- 2 tables or 2 chairs
- 30 cm (12 in.) masking tape
- an egg timer or watch
- toy cars

You have ten minutes to meet this challenge. (Set egg timer.)

1. Position the tables or chairs a meter (a yard) apart.

2. From the materials provided and in ten minutes, design a bridge that spans the gap between the tables or chairs.

3. When the time is up, start loading your bridge with cars. See how many cars your bridge can hold before it collapses. (You can make it really interesting by adding "wind," in the form of a fan.)

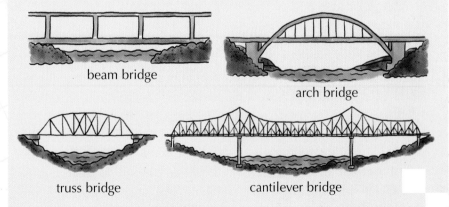

beam bridge

arch bridge

truss bridge

cantilever bridge

SOUTH FORK DAM

The story of the South Fork Dam failure has all the makings of a movie — a club for the rich, a huge storm, a dam failure and the destruction of a working-class town.

Dam engineering principles are simple: A dam must be watertight and stable, with a controlled outlet to safely get rid of excess water. The South Fork Dam, built near Johnstown, Pennsylvania between 1838 and 1853, was an embankment dam, made of mounded-up earth, boulders and clay. It had a stone culvert (small tunnel), controlled by valves, to discharge extra water. On the dam's east end was a 26 m (85 ft.) wide spillway. If the water behind the dam got too high, it was supposed to overflow and pour down the spillway.

The morning after the South Fork Dam burst, Johnstown's streets were heaped with mud and rubble three stories high.

From the beginning, the dam had problems, mostly small leaks and cracks. The South Fork Hunting and Fishing Club bought it in 1879 and used it to create an artificial, trout-stocked lake.

Death Moves Down the Valley

On May 31, 1889, after a night of heavy rain, the dam broke. A wave of water shot down the valley leading to Johnstown, a city of 30 000 people.

The dam ruptured at 3:10 p.m., and the water hit town at 4:07 p.m. At times the wave reached a height of 12 m (40 ft.) and a speed of 65 km/h (40 m.p.h). And, because it had already raced for miles, the water churned with debris.

In just ten minutes, almost everything in the wave's path was destroyed. Houses exploded and trees were uprooted. Johnstown's stone bridge held back debris, including the bodies of animals and people, allowing some residents to escape. But when the water, coated with oil from the waste, caught fire, eighty trapped people perished. In all, more than 2000 people died.

This bridge caught debris, including tangled barbed wire that ensnared animals and people.

Dam Failure

What caused the South Fork Dam failure? Three things. First, the culvert's valves were shut off, so water was not being discharged. Secondly, the club had built a trap across the dam's spillway to keep fish in the lake. The trap became clogged with debris, and the water had nowhere to drain. Thirdly, the dam had an unrepaired sag that weakened the structure. Together, the three problems spelled disaster for the people of Johnstown.

- **The South Fork Dam stretched 280 m (918 ft.) across a valley and was more than 22 m (72 ft.) high.**
- **The world's biggest dam, the controversial Three Gorges Dam in China, will be completed in 2009. It will span 2.2 km (1.4 mi.) across the Yangtze River and tower about 175 m (575 ft.).**

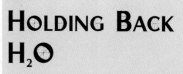

HOLDING BACK H₂O

A dam's job is to manage flowing water. But water can be pushy! So engineers have had to come up with super strong structures to hold back the water.

Embankment dams are made of earth, boulders and clay. The South Fork Dam was an embankment dam.

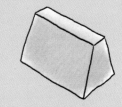

Gravity dams rely on their huge mass to keep the water back.

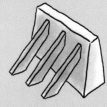

Buttress dams rely on buttresses (note the triangular shape) to push back against the water.

Arch dams are curved. The shape allows them to be relatively thin yet still strong.

PANAMA CANAL

A jungle, an untamed river and disease — a formidable trio that made building a canal across the country of Panama an almost impossible dream.

Construction was impossible for a French company already famous for building the Suez Canal in Egypt. They had tried it and failed in the late 1880s. The Americans took over in 1904, and it took ten years to complete the 82 km (51 mi.) long canal through Panama. For ships, it was a huge improvement — instead of traveling around the tip of South America, they could travel across Panama and shave 14 400 km (9000 mi.) from trips between New York and San Francisco.

How did engineers pull off this amazing feat? Window screens, for starters.

It took four years to build the Panama Canal's locks.

Little Insects, Big Problems

During the French canal effort, yellow fever and malaria killed thousands of workers. There's definitely a problem with a building project when three out of four workers die from disease.

When the Americans took over, they ran into the same problem. In fact, most of the American workers booked passage home. That's where the window screens came in. The canal's Chief Sanitary Officer, Dr. William Gorgas, believed in a new theory — mosquitoes spread the diseases.

His team first attacked the mosquito that carries yellow fever. It likes to live near humans, so Dr. Gorgas targeted Panama City. All standing water — a great place for mosquitoes to lay eggs — was eradicated, and mosquito

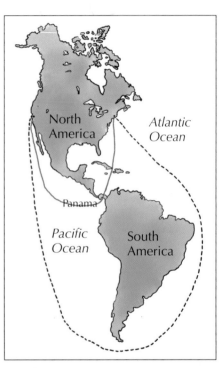

The dotted line shows the route ships had to take before the Panama Canal was built. The red line shows the new, faster route.

netting and running water were provided to workers. Windows and doors were screened, and in a matter of months yellow fever was wiped out in the city.

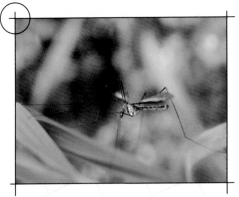

Attacking malaria-carrying mosquitoes, however, was like going after a jungle of beasts, Dr. Gorgas said. They live just about everywhere, and the malaria they carry kills more people than yellow fever. After researching the mosquito's habits, the team drained swamps, cleared vegetation, sprayed oil on standing water, released minnows to eat mosquito larvae and bred spiders, ants and lizards to feed on the adult insects. Malaria cases dropped.

With disease under control, Chief Engineer John Stevens turned to keeping the workers happy. While half of the 24 000 laborers were digging a giant "ditch" across Panama, the other half were constructing towns complete with houses, dining halls, hospitals, hotels, churches and schools for workers and their families. They even started a baseball league.

The Big Ditch

Some canals are literally big ditches. Ships sail in one end and out the other. But a different solution was needed in Panama. A "lake and lock" design was adopted. Panama's Chagres River would be dammed to create a new lake, called Gatún Lake, in the interior. A series of locks would raise ships from the Atlantic Ocean to the lake level. Ships would cross Gatún Lake, then descend another set of locks to the Pacific Ocean. It would be a bit like climbing steps, crossing a field and going down another set of steps on the other side.

The digging began. Dynamite was used to clear rock and loosen the rock-hard clay of the canal. Then rock and soil (called "spoil") were dug out and loaded onto trains for removal.

The biggest challenge was the steep, landslide-prone Culebra Cut. There, spoil trains traveled to different levels to haul out about 76 million m³ (100 million cu. yd.) of rock and soil. That's enough to fill the Empire State Building almost 76 times. When the digging was done, the 14 km (8.75 mi.) long Culebra Cut looked like the Grand Canyon. At places its sides were as high as a 25-story building. Some of its spoil was used to build dams, a breakwater in Panama Bay, a townsite and a military base.

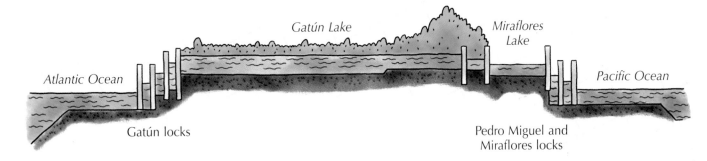

Gatún Lake

Miraflores Lake

Atlantic Ocean

Pacific Ocean

Gatún locks

Pedro Miguel and Miraflores locks

Layin' the Locks

The locks — all twelve of them — are considered an engineering triumph. They were the first to be operated by electricity and the first made of a relatively new material: concrete.

The canal actually has two "traffic lanes" — six locks for ships going from the Pacific to the Atlantic and another six locks for ships going from the Atlantic to the Pacific.

When entering from the Atlantic side, three locks lift ships about 26 m (85 ft.) to Gatún Lake. From Gatún Lake, the ships are lowered 9.5 m (31 ft.) through one lock to Miraflores Lake. Two more locks at Miraflores lower ships to the Pacific Ocean.

The locks during construction (above) and today.

HOW A LOCK WORKS

A lock is just two sets of doors with room big enough for a ship between them. Here's how a ship goes down through a lock.

1. A ship enters a lock and the gates close behind it.

2. Water drains out through sluices to lower the water level in the lock.

3. The gates in front open and the ship sails out.

Commemoration Exercises - Gatun Locks, Panama Canal.

Ships today are much bigger than this one from 1939.

A (Very Quiet) Drumroll, Please

The first trip through the canal by a self-propelled, ocean-going vessel took place on January 7, 1914. The *Alexandre La Valley,* an old French crane boat, went from the Atlantic to the Pacific.

The Panama Canal was officially opened on August 15, 1914. Beginning with the French initiative, it had taken more than half a billion dollars and tens of thousands of workers to build the canal. Many thousands died. Despite all this, the news of its opening was met with little hoopla — World War I had just erupted.

- The Panama Canal can handle about fifty ships per day. On average, it takes a ship eight to ten hours to pass completely through the canal.
- Ships pay a toll — based on cargo volume and measurements — to use the canal. The highest toll ever was $165,235.58, paid by the cruise ship *Rhapsody of the Seas* on April 15, 1998. The lowest toll was thirty-six cents, paid by Richard Halliburton who swam the canal in 1928.

More than 880 000 vessels have passed through the Panama Canal since it was officially opened in 1914.

CHERNOBYL

A flawed design and an experiment that went wrong caused explosions at the Chernobyl nuclear power plant in Ukraine on April 26, 1986. The explosions released more lethal radiation than the two atomic bombs dropped on Japan in 1945.

In a nuclear reactor, energy from a nuclear reaction (splitting uranium atoms) heats water, which turns into steam, which drives turbines to produce power. Fuel rods power the nuclear reaction, but if left unchecked they overheat. Most reactors use water to cool the fuel rods. The Soviet-designed Chernobyl reactor used graphite. In a graphite-cooled reactor, things can get out of control fast and the graphite can ignite.

On April 26, plant managers began an experiment. They wanted to see if a winding-down turbine could generate enough electricity to last for the forty to fifty seconds it would take for back-up diesel generators to take over.

Reactor no. 4's power was cut. Warning lights blinked, but the automatic shut down system was disconnected because the managers wanted to complete the experiment. In seconds, the reactor went out of control. Steam built up finally causing two explosions that ripped the roof off the reactor.

The area around Chernobyl is a wasteland filled with ghost towns. More than 180 000 people were evacuated from villages and towns. No people live — and nothing is farmed — in the area around the nuclear reactor.

Radioactive Death

Radioactive material shot skyward and fires broke out. Radiation poisoning killed thirty-one people outright. Many were firefighters, some so contaminated they were buried in lead coffins. But radiation travels on the wind and can continue to kill for years. No one is sure how many people have died so far and what the final death toll will be.

- It took firefighters in helicopters two weeks to douse the reactor fire. It took more than six months to entomb the reactor in a lead and concrete sarcophagus.
- Chernobyl's radiation rained across borders, affecting many countries — including Ireland, more than 2500 km (1550 mi.) away.

BHOPAL

On December 2, 1984, workers at a Bhopal, India, pesticide plant ran for their lives. Poisonous chemical fumes were blowing south, straight towards Bhopal, a city of 900 000.

Bhopal's Union Carbide pesticide plant made the chemical MIC. It reacts violently with water. On that night, 500 L (130 gal.) of water seeped into an MIC storage tank. The tanks cracked and 40 t (44 tn.) of MIC escaped and spread 8 km (5 mi.). Some people died as they slept and some as they fled.

Five Deadly Errors

The leak became a disaster when five back-up systems failed:

1. The refrigeration unit used to keep MIC cool (and less likely to overheat and expand if contaminated) had been turned off five months earlier.
2. A storage tank for excess MIC was already full.
3. A gas scrubber, designed to neutralize escaping gas, didn't work.
4. The flare tower, which burned off escaping MIC from the gas scrubber, wasn't working.
5. Spray from fire truck hoses couldn't reach the escaping gas fumes.

Shoddy Standards

The company's poor standards for maintenance, safety procedures and worker training caused the Bhopal plant failure. More than 7000 people died and thousands more were injured.

While a similar — though less deadly — accident at a sister plant in the U.S. led to changes in American environmental and worker safety laws, in India changes have been slow.

Stinging eyes were the first warning sign for many people living near Bhopal's Union Carbide plant. Today, twenty years later, many are still affected by lung damage.

APOLLO 13

The Apollo 13 *launch*

"Houston, we've had a problem here." Scary words to hear from astronauts hurtling through space to the moon.

Apollo 13 was NASA's third mission to land astronauts on the moon. Fifty-six hours into the flight, astronauts Jim Lovell, Fred Haise and Jack Swigert heard a loud bang. Liquid oxygen tank no. 2 in the service module had exploded. This was quickly followed by a loss of pressure in tank no. 1 and the loss of *Apollo*'s fuel cells. Without the fuel cells, the supply of electricity, light and water available to the astronauts plummeted.

The mission's objectives immediately changed — get back to Earth, fast!

Lunar Lifeboat

To save power, the crew moved into the cramped lunar module (LM), the vehicle they had hoped to land on the moon. They fired the LM's descent engine to put themselves on a "free return trajectory" that would have them pass around the back of the moon and return to Earth.

When it came time to re-enter Earth's atmosphere, the plan was for the astronauts to move back into the main part of the spacecraft, the command module (CM). They would need its heat shield to protect them.

It was a great plan. But there was one big hitch. The LM was not designed to sustain three astronauts for the ninety hours needed to get home. To stretch resources, the crew rationed fuel, water and food.

All went well, until carbon dioxide levels began to climb, as the three astronauts breathed in the cramped quarters. The LM's filters, which scrubbed carbon dioxide out of the air, were just about used up. No problem: they would borrow filters from the CM. But that turned out to be a big problem. The LM's filters were round. The CM's were square.

Apollo 13 *astronauts Haise, Lovell and Swigert (left to right).*

Quick thinking and duct tape averted disaster. With materials on board — plastic bags, cardboard and duct tape — astronauts fitted a square filter canister into a round opening.

Four days after the explosion, astronauts Lovell, Haise and Swigert splashed down in the Pacific Ocean. In one piece and breathing easy.

Duct tape and ingenuity fixed a filter problem and saved lives.

Apollo 13's Command Module landed only 6.4 km (4 mi.) from the recovery ship in the Pacific Ocean.

Internal Bomb

The problem with tank no. 2 started long before *Apollo 13* left the ground. The tank had originally been installed for the *Apollo 10* mission.

Before being installed on *Apollo 13*, the tank was tested and deemed safe. But *Apollo 13* had been rewired. The old tank ran on a lower voltage than the newly rewired spacecraft. Pre-launch testing damaged the tank's wiring insulation, and when the fans were turned on during the mission, wires sparked. Insulation caught fire and — *bang!* — the tank exploded.

NASA made three important changes on subsequent Apollo missions: the oxygen tanks were modified, a third liquid-oxygen tank was added and a back-up battery was installed.

APOLLO 1 FIRE

During a launch pad test in 1967, fire swept through the command module of *Apollo 1* and killed three astronauts. A short circuit had sparked a fire.

NASA made changes — 1341 in all — to all Apollo spacecrafts after the tragedy. The wiring changes saved *Apollo 13*. When *Apollo 13* astronauts powered up the CM for re-entry into Earth's atmosphere, condensation clung to everything, but nothing sparked. It did, however, rain on the three heroes.

CANADARM

Stranded in space? Need a helping hand? Look no further than Canadarm. With the catchy official name of "Shuttle Remote Manipulator System," this robot arm has helped astronauts fix the Hubble Space Telescope, knock ice from a space shuttle's clogged waste-water vent and build the International Space Station. Canadarm is so handy, space shuttles rarely leave home without one.

Testing, Testing

NASA needed the equivalent of a bionic arm to load and unload cargo in space and to help astronauts do repair work. The arm had to be lightweight, sturdy, nimble, easy to control both manually and automatically, reliable and reusable. No small task! NASA officials knew what they wanted — they just weren't sure it could be built.

Canadian aerospace engineers took up the challenge in 1974. They designed an arm made of a carbon composite, a lightweight but strong material. It would work like a human arm, with joints at the shoulder, elbow and wrists, and small motors instead of muscles. Its hand would be a snare system that would close around objects like a high-tech lasso. The end result was an arm that could move much like your arm and be operated by an astronaut at the controls.

That's how the arm was designed to work, but would it? The only way to find out was to build and test. Redesign, build and test. And then test some more. At first, models were used. But once the arm went full scale, testing got tricky. The arm was for in-space use. On Earth, it couldn't even support its own weight. So a special rig had to cradle the arm while it was tested.

In November 1981, Canadarm made its debut on the space shuttle *Columbia*. The verdict: reliable, reusable — and a big help in space. Since then, Canadarm2, an even bigger robot arm, has been built. Junior and Senior worked together to help build the International Space Station. And while Canadarm2 has suffered a glitch or two, none of the Canadarms — four in all — has failed in more than fifty missions. Talk about handy!

Testing, testing, testing made Canadarm a real performer in space.

- A Canadarm was destroyed in the 1986 *Challenger* explosion.
- Canadarm is 15 m (50 ft.) long and weighs a mere 410 kg (905 lb.), yet in space it can lift something as heavy as a bus full of people.

THE DEPTHS OF ENGINEERING

Psst! Want to see some deep sea vents? Ask *Alvin*. Built in 1964, this deep-sea submersible plunges scientists to extreme ocean depths. Without it, researchers would never have found hydrothermal vents, a missing nuclear bomb or seen the wrecked *Titanic*.

Alvin can operate at 4500 m (14 764 ft.) below sea level. A titanium hull keeps the three-person submersible from collapsing under the extreme pressure. But its two hydraulic-powered robotic arms — each with a 188 cm (74 in.) reach — are the real stars. Each arm can lift up to 68 kg (150 lbs). The arms are used to collect live specimens and geological samples. Attached sensors take chemical readings of the environment.

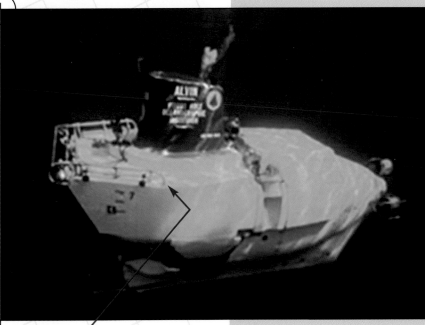

Submersible Alvin

HUBBLE SPACE TELESCOPE

The Hubble Space Telescope gets its eyesight fixed by astronauts using the Canadarm.

April 24, 1990. What a day! What a quest! Our view of the universe was about to change with the launch of the Hubble Space Telescope. Finally, an orbiting telescope that would let us see deep into space!

But when the Hubble was launched … disappointment. Who knew the universe was so, well, fuzzy?

The Challenge

Astronomers knew what they wanted — a telescope and a spacecraft in one.

As a spacecraft, Hubble would have a thermal blanket for protection from extreme heat and cold. Two solar arrays (panels) would provide 3000 watts of power — only enough to power thirty household lights here on Earth, but enough to keep Hubble going and recharge its batteries.

As a telescope, Hubble was to have incredible vision, mostly because of its location in space. Up there, there's no pesky atmosphere to get in the way as there is on Earth. Instructions would be beamed to Hubble's four antennae, via one of five orbiting satellites. The instructions would guide Hubble's "eye" to focus on certain targets. Gyroscopes would keep Hubble steady for the long exposures it needs to take pictures of faraway, dim objects.

Hubble

Billion Dollar Boo-Boo

Astronomers and engineers had high expectations. But — oops! — the first images Hubble sent back were blurry. The boo-boo was a flawed primary mirror. It was slightly misshapen because the "null corrector" used to test the curvature of the mirrors was made to the wrong specifications. As a result, when the mirror was being made, it, too, came out slightly "off spec."

To add to the trouble, engineers failed to check how the mirror worked with the other instruments. Instead they relied on computer simulations. So Hubble was in orbit before anyone noticed the problem. Even though the curvature of the mirror was only off by $\frac{1}{50}$ the width of a human hair, it was enough to give Hubble poor eyesight.

The Eagle Nebula, as captured by Hubble.

- What is the size of a bus and orbits Earth every ninety-seven minutes? The Hubble Space Telescope.
- In just ten years, Hubble orbited the Earth 58 400 times.
- The Hubble Space Telescope was named after astronomer Edwin Hubble, who, in the 1920s, proved that a whole universe existed beyond the Milky Way.

Putting on Glasses

In 1993, the space shuttle *Endeavour* crew installed corrective "lenses" to fix Hubble's optics. Five pairs of new, redesigned mirrors, housed inside a telephone booth–sized instrument, were attached to Hubble. The mirrors corrected the "vision" of one camera and two spectrographs — just like glasses perched on someone's nose. Canadarm (page 42) helped make the repair. The fix was a success.

Since then, Hubble has revealed planets orbiting distant stars, found evidence of black holes and measured the age of the universe, a "young" 13 to 14 billion years. When Hubble "retires," perhaps in 2010, it will have allowed us to see where no one has ever seen before.

WORLD TRADE CENTER

On September 11, 2001, terrorists crashed passenger airplanes into two of New York's World Trade Center (WTC) towers. More than 2700 people died when the towers collapsed. The destruction and the deaths were shocking. The buildings, after all, had been strong and stable. But engineers know that all structures, even the strongest, have the potential to collapse.

Not everyone wanted the towering giants in the first place. Politicians cobbled the plan together in the 1960s in a bid to revitalize lower Manhattan, a decaying old port. Some called the WTC the "unconquerable Frankenstein" because every time the plans hit a snag, the complex just kept getting bigger. Soon the plan for the complex had expanded to a total of seven buildings.

PEACE

The Twin Towers at its center would each rise 110 stories, making them the world's tallest skyscrapers at the time.

Building that high and that big — the complex would have 930 000 m² (10 million sq. ft.) of office space — was a challenge. Architect Minoru Yamasaki and engineers Leslie Robertson and John Skilling looked to a new design, the "tube."

The Twin Tubes

Traditionally, skyscrapers had a skeleton of steel supporting a curtain wall. But this design requires support columns every 6 to 9 m (20 to 30 ft.), which take up valuable office space. The tube design changed all that. Closely spaced steel columns were placed at only the building's central core

The Twin Towers were an important part of New York City's identity — and its skyline.

and outer walls. There were no support columns in between. Space-hogging elevators and stairs were also tucked into the central core. The floors were concrete, held up by steel trusses, which are lighter than the usual girders or beams. The bottom line: Tube buildings could reach higher, resist wind and natural forces efficiently, cost less to build and provide more office space. The Twin Towers of the WTC would be tubes, spacious but sturdy.

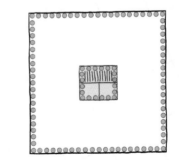

A traditional building has columns evenly spaced. A tube design has columns only at the outer walls and the central core.

Going up

All skyscrapers sway, and at 110 stories, the Twin Towers might sway enough to make people motion sick. To deal with the movement, the engineers developed a novel system of dampers for the towers. The dampers — more than 10 000 for each tower — would absorb the wind-induced motion, making life at the top a more stable affair.

The elevators were another innovation. Speedy express elevators would deposit passengers at the "skylobbies" on the 44th and 78th floors. From there they would take other elevators to their destinations. Each tower also had one elevator that went from top to bottom.

The towers were built over a period of seven years. They were officially opened in 1973. And the design worked. The North Tower even withstood a bomb attack in the parking basement in 1993. Then came September 11.

Towering Targets

The first hijacked plane hit the WTC's North Tower at 8:46 a.m. Onlookers couldn't believe their eyes. The second plane smashed into the South Tower $16\frac{1}{2}$ minutes later.

More than half the support columns were severed on the floors where the planes hit. At first, the weight of the upper floors was transferred around the gashes to the columns that remained intact. The towers absorbed the impact, and people began to evacuate.

There was worse to come. Ignited by full tanks of jet fuel, fires raged to at least 600°C (1100°F). The steel support columns softened. The lightweight floor trusses attached to them sagged and tore away from the columns. The floors collapsed, each one adding more weight to the ones below. The North Tower stood for 103 minutes, the South Tower for 56 minutes. It only took about ten seconds for each building to fall once the collapse had begun.

Engineering for the Unexpected

After the tragedy, engineers asked one question right away: why did the South Tower — hit second — fall first? One theory was that the fire insulation was at fault. Some noted that the insulation on the South Tower's burning floors was half as thick as on the North Tower's. Others said the insulation was knocked off when the planes hit.

Maybe more insulation would have kept the towers standing longer, allowing more people to escape. Maybe 103 and 56 minutes of strength is a feat in itself. The Twin Towers' performance under such devastating circumstances can be viewed either way, as a feat or a failure. One thing is for sure, engineers design tall buildings differently since September 11.

Skyscrapers across the U.S. were modified and new buildings were redesigned to be sturdier. In

- Fazlur R. Khan, a civil engineer, is considered the "father" of tubular design. He designed the 442 m (1450 ft.) Sears Tower, using an improved tube design. It's the world's second tallest skyscraper.
- Express elevators zoomed up the Twin Towers at a speed of 8 m (26 ft.) per second.

New York, Times Square Tower, built in 2002, had extra steel plating 2.5 cm (1 in.) thick welded on at crucial points. New building designs place emergency stairs farther apart, and a building's core is more likely to be made from steel and concrete for more strength, not steel and quick-to-burn drywall.

As with other examples of feats and failures, engineers have learned many lessons from the

tragedy of September 11. Engineers warn, however, that building against terrorist attacks is a never-ending battle. No matter how big or strong the structure, someone may find a way to turn a feat into a failure.

SKYSCRAPING COLLISIONS

Before the WTC was even built, an opponent to the plan placed a big newspaper advertisement that featured a drawing of a commercial plane about to slam into one of the Twin Towers. It was an eerie case of foreshadowing and a reminder of an earlier disaster.

In 1945, fog caused a B-25 bomber pilot to become confused. When he dropped down from the clouds, his plane was surrounded by skyscrapers. After missing a few, his plane slammed into the Empire State Building's 79th floor. The bomber's fuel tank exploded, and fourteen people died.

Debris from the top of the towers hit the ground at an estimated speed of 162 km/h (100 mph).

MURPHY'S LAW

Captain Edward Murphy, an engineer with the U.S. Air Force, coined the saying known as Murphy's Law: If anything can go wrong, it will. It's a saying that engineers pay attention to because it's what separates the feats and the failures.

Captain Murphy was involved with acceleration and deceleration experiments at Edwards Air Force Base in California in the 1940s and 1950s. Dr. John Paul Stapp, who designed the experiments, rode on a rocket-powered sled that accelerated to more than 1000 km/h (630 mph). The G-forces (gravity forces) Stapp experienced were enormous — an unpleasant experience, to put it mildly. But worse, when Stapp staggered off the sled after one session, all the sensors measuring the G-forces read 0. All that for nothing!

Murphy checked the sensors and discovered that every single one had been installed the wrong way. He exclaimed, "If there are two or more ways to do something and one of those results in a catastrophe, then someone will do it that way." Today we've shortened the saying.

Engineers interpret it as: "If you want things to go right, pay attention to everything that can go wrong." In other words, test, retest and test again, imagine every possible disaster and whatever you do, have a back-up plan or two. Oh yeah, and learn from past feats and failures.

Dr. John Paul Stapp in the process of testing the sled, which led to the saying, "If anything can go wrong, it will."

Glossary

The definitions you see here apply to the words as they are used in this book.

aerodynamics: How air or fluids flow around an object, and the interaction of the object with that flow. Engineers test vehicles, bridges and other structures for their aerodynamic effects and properties as they move through a fluid or a gas.

beam: A support used in buildings and other structures to carry loads and span distances. For example, a house has beams under its floor. They span from wall to wall and support the weight of people and things. Beams can be made of almost anything, but wood, steel and concrete are the most popular materials.

caisson: A watertight chamber that allows people to dig underwater or through wet soil. Caissons hold the water back to enable construction.

canal lock: A waterway structure with a gate at either end that permits the raising or lowering of ships to different water levels.

compression: A pushing force that tends to squash. A building's columns are in compression.

curtain wall: An outer wall of a building that is "hung" from the structural frame. It is only a covering and generally does not support weight.

engineer of record: The lead engineer on a project, responsible for any changes to the original design.

girder: A large beam used in structures to support weight from above. When different sizes of beams transfer loads onto one another in a structure, the larger beams are often referred to as girders.

graphite: A form of carbon.

hydraulic jack: A device for lifting or pushing heavy things, using oil pressure. For example, a hydraulic jack can be used to lift cars for repair work.

radiation: Energy given off or transmitted as particles or rays.

tension: A pulling force that tends to stretch. For example, a stretched elastic is under tension.

turbine: An engine with blades arranged so that the energy of moving fluids or gases causes the blades to turn, or rotate. In power plants, this rotation of the blades is used to generate power.

truss: A supporting framework made of beams, girders or bars, usually in the shape of a triangle or combination of triangles. Trusses are often used for long spans, such as bridges, and heavy loads, such as roofs.

INDEX